Let's Visit the Zoo

written by Lori C. Froeb

reviewed by Donald E. Moore III, PhD

Silver Dolphin

San Diego, California

Welcome to the zoo! My name is Emily and I'm a zookeeper.

As a kid, I loved animals and enjoyed learning all about them. I knew that I wanted to take care of them one day. Now, as a zookeeper, my job is to make sure all the animals at the zoo are comfortable, well fed, happy, and healthy. Working with animals is a dream come true!

What is a zoo? It's a place where people can come to see animals from all over the world. We try to make the animals feel at home by making their zoo **habitat** similar to where they would live in the wild. Some of our animals are endangered. This means that there are not many of them left in the world. We work to help make sure they don't become **extinct**. When an animal becomes extinct, it is gone forever.

Would you like to meet the animals at the zoo?
I would love to tell you all about them!

A World of Animals

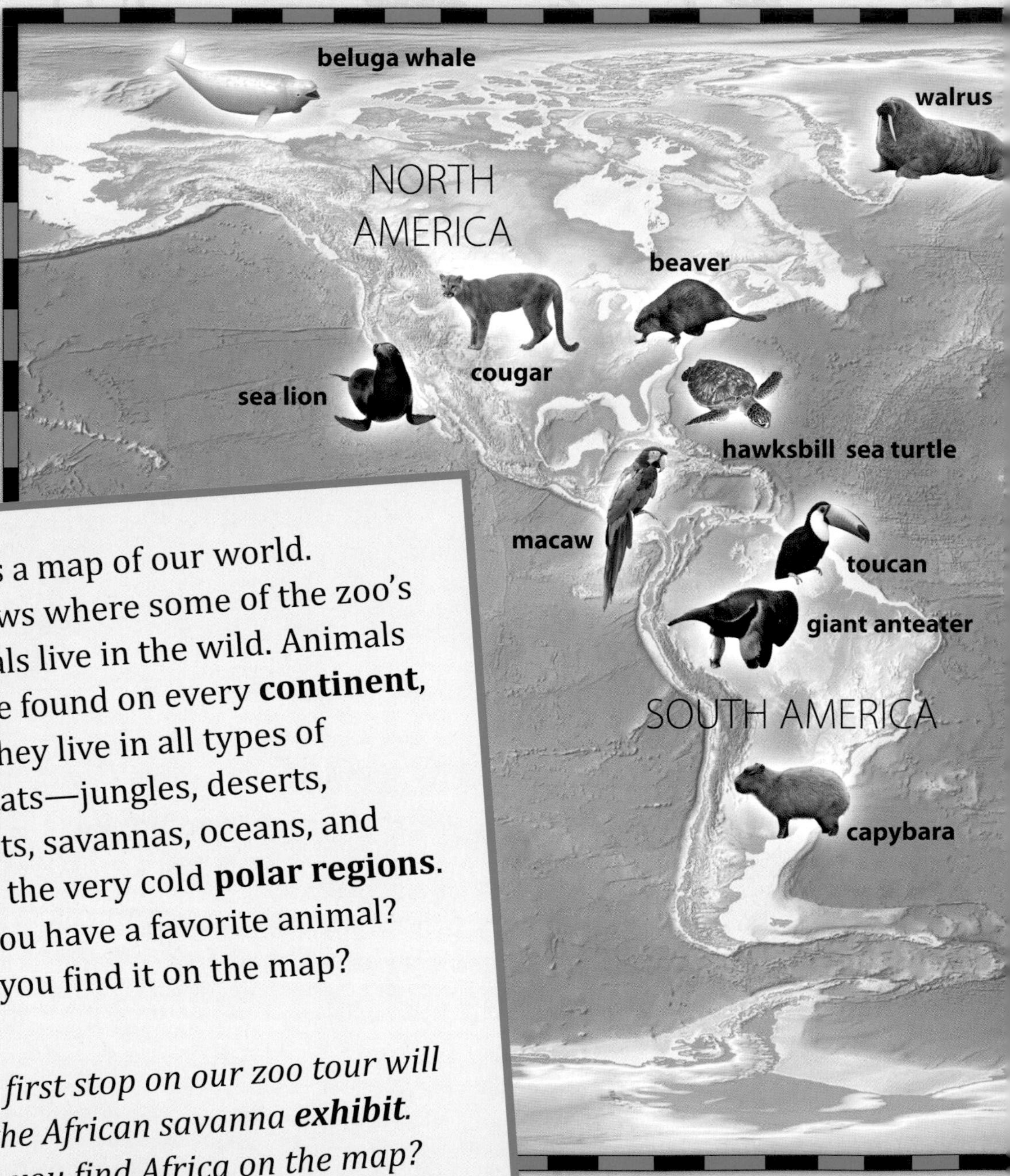

beluga whale

walrus

NORTH AMERICA

beaver

cougar

sea lion

hawksbill sea turtle

macaw

toucan

giant anteater

SOUTH AMERICA

capybara

This is a map of our world. It shows where some of the zoo's animals live in the wild. Animals can be found on every **continent**, and they live in all types of habitats—jungles, deserts, forests, savannas, oceans, and even the very cold **polar regions**. Do you have a favorite animal? Can you find it on the map?

The first stop on our zoo tour will be the African savanna **exhibit**. *Can you find Africa on the map?*

puffin

polar bear

ASIA

EUROPE

snow leopard

panda

AFRICA

hippopotamus

tiger

lion

orangutan

elephant

sloth bear

lemur

Komodo dragon

reef shark

koala

cheetah

AUSTRALIA

platypus

penguin

ANTARCTICA

The African Savanna

Welcome to the African savanna! Savannas are open, grassy areas that are scattered with trees. African savannas have a long dry season followed by a long wet season. Herds of animals follow the rains so they will have water to drink. Who lives on the savanna?

▲ Lion
These big cats live together in a group called a pride. The female lions hunt for the food while the male lion protects the group. Only male lions have manes.

◀ African Elephant
An elephant's trunk is used for many things—breathing, sniffing, drinking, spraying, picking up things, and grabbing food.

▲ Hippopotamus
The name *hippopotamus* means "river horse" in Greek. This is the perfect name for an animal that spends most of its time in the water.

▲ Zebra

Why do zebras have stripes? Scientists think the stripes are a type of **camouflage** that helps to protect zebras from **predators**. When many zebras run together, all those stripes confuse predators so they can't pick out one zebra to attack.

Warthog ▶

Even though this warthog looks ferocious, it would much rather run and hide than fight. It backs into a burrow to hide with its tusks facing out for protection.

▲ Giraffe

Meet the tallest land animal alive! A giraffe's neck is long, and so is its tongue. Both help the giraffe grab tasty leaves from tall trees.

Our next stop is the Amazon rain forest exhibit. Many colorful animals are waiting for you!

Animals of the Amazon

The Amazon tropical rain forest, or jungle, is in South America. It is home to thousands of different **species** of animals. There is nowhere else on earth where you can find so many different creatures living in one area. Like all tropical rain forests, the Amazon is warm and wet. About 100 inches of rain falls there every year!

◀ Toucan

The toucan's beak is half as long as its body. While it may look heavy, it isn't. Inside, it looks like a sponge full of little air pockets—making it very light. It comes in handy for picking hard-to-reach fruit.

Blue Poison Dart Frog ▶

This little frog's skin is poisonous. A predator that tries to eat it will get very sick—or even die. This frog's bright colors warn predators that it is poisonous.

Scarlet Macaw ▶

These birds wear almost all the colors of the rainbow! Macaws are large—almost two feet long. They have loud squawks that they use to call other macaws from miles away.

Giant Anteater ▶

Can you guess what an anteater eats? Ants! It doesn't have any teeth, so it collects ants by sticking out its long, sticky tongue. It can eat up to 30,000 ants and termites a day.

◀ Three-toed Sloth

Sloths are animals that love to hang around. Most of their time is spent snoozing—up to 20 hours a day! When they are awake, they move very slowly using their strong front legs to "walk" upside down along the branches.

Piranha ▶

Piranhas are little fish with big teeth that like to eat meat. They usually eat dead or weak animals that fall in the Amazon River, but will sometimes attack and eat live animals.

Let's move on to another exhibit that will take us across the Pacific Ocean to Asia. It's where our tigers are. But what other animals live there? Let's find out!

Amazing Asia

Asia is the largest continent in the world. It has many different habitats—mountains, deserts, rain forests, and even polar regions. The animals here come from places like India, China, Nepal, and Bangladesh. Do you recognize any of these animals from Asia?

Indian Rhinoceros
This rhino from India has only one horn. It is made of keratin—the same stuff your hair and fingernails are made of.

Giant Panda
These bears live in the cool bamboo forests of China. Bamboo is their favorite food. To chew the tough stems, pandas have very strong mouth muscles and big grinding teeth.

Sloth Bear ▶

These shaggy bears love to feast on termites. A hungry bear will scratch open a termite nest and then suck up the insects through its snout.

◀ Komodo Dragon

These giant meat-eating lizards are the largest in the world and live on the islands of Indonesia. They can weigh up to 300 pounds!

Bengal Tiger ▶

Tigers are found in many parts of Asia. They are the only big cats that have stripes. Not all Bengal tigers are orange—some have white coats!

Are you ready to meet some unusual animals?
Australia is full of them. That is our next stop!

Weird and Wonderful Australia

Australia is an island continent that is home to fascinating creatures that are not found anywhere else. Many of the most poisonous animals on earth live there. Our zoo doesn't have any of those, but we do have some interesting creatures from Australia. Let's meet them!

◀ Koala

These fuzzy animals live in the branches of the eucalyptus forests. The leaves are the only things they will eat. When they aren't eating, they are sleeping—up to 18 hours a day!

Kangaroo ▶

Kangaroos and koalas are **marsupials**. That means that their babies do most of their growing in the mother's pouch. A baby kangaroo is called a joey.

Platypus ▶

What has webbed feet, a mouth like a duck's, a tail like a beaver's, and is covered in fur? It's a platypus! This is one of only two **mammals** that lay eggs.

◀ Tasmanian Devil

It might be small, but the Tasmanian devil is ferocious! Its mouth is strong enough to bite through metal wire. It's loud, too! The screaming sound it makes is probably how it got its name.

Echidna ▶

The long snout of this mammal is its mouth and nose. It uses its long, sticky tongue to slurp up ants and termites from their nests. Like the platypus, the echidna lays eggs rather than giving birth to its young.

Grab your coat and let's go! We are going to visit the animals that live in the chilliest places on earth!

It's Cool to Be Polar

All the animals you see here live in the polar regions of the Arctic and Antarctica. There is often snow and ice where they live, and it is usually cold. It would be hard for us to live there, but it's perfect for these polar animals!

Puffin
These little birds are excellent swimmers. By "flying" underwater (and diving as deep as 200 feet), a puffin can catch and hold more than 20 fish in its beak!

Polar Bear
Polar bears spend most of their lives on ice. To stay warm, they have several inches of fat, or blubber, on their bodies. Under all that white fur, their skin is black!

Arctic Fox ▶

This tricky fox uses its amazing hearing to find small animals moving under deep snow. When it finds one, the fox pounces with its paws to break through the snow and grab its **prey**.

◀ Walrus

A walrus's tusks can be over three feet long and are used to help it climb out of the water onto the ice. The tusks are also used for digging for clams and for fighting with other walruses.

Chinstrap Penguin ▶

After laying two eggs in a rocky nest, the female penguins take turns with the male penguins keeping the eggs warm until they hatch. These birds live in Antarctica.

Many of our exhibits are grouped by a type of animal instead of a habitat. Let me take you to my favorite exhibit—the primates! Do you know what a primate is?

Primates

Do you recognize some of these animals? They are all primates. Primates are a group of animals that includes apes, monkeys, lemurs, and also humans. All primates have five fingers and can use their thumbs to grasp and hold things. Both of their eyes both face forward. Primates also have large brains for their size—making them very smart!

▲ Orangutan

This ape's arms stretch up to seven feet across and are perfect for swinging from branch to branch. Orangutans are found only on the islands of Borneo and Sumatra, in Southeast Asia. Their name means "man of the forest."

▲ Gorilla

Meet the largest primate! Gorillas are apes that live in the forests of Africa. Each night, a gorilla makes a nest out of branches and leaves to sleep in!

Tarsier ▶

This little primate from Southeast Asia has huge eyes that are great for seeing in the dark as it hunts the insects and small lizards it eats. The tarsier can fit in the palm of your hand.

Ring-tailed ▶ Lemur

Like skunks, these primates use smells to talk to each other. A lemur can tell if a scent was left by a male or female lemur, and if it was healthy or sick! The lemur lives on the island of Madagascar, off the coast of Africa.

▲
Chimpanzee

These apes are the closest living relatives of humans. Chimpanzees use many different tools. They often use rocks to open nuts, and also poke sticks into termite nests to get the bugs inside. They live in Africa.

Pygmy Marmoset ▶

This tiny monkey from South America weighs just 3.5 ounces. Its favorite food is tree gum, a type of sap, which it slurps after chewing a hole in the bark.

Do you like snakes? Lizards? What about turtles?
You can find these in the reptile exhibit!

Reptiles

Reptiles are cold-blooded animals. This means their bodies are the same temperature as their surroundings. They must lie in the sun to warm up and move into the shade or water to cool off. Reptiles have a hard shell or scaly skin, and their brains are small for their size. Most lay eggs. Crocodiles and alligators, turtles and tortoises, snakes, and lizards are all reptiles!

▲ Panther Chameleon

This chameleon from Madagascar has unusual skin! It can change colors to show the chameleon's mood, and as a reaction to temperature and light.

Leopard Tortoise ▶

Like many large tortoises, the leopard tortoise can live 100 years or more. It gets its name from the patterns on its shell. It lives in Africa.

Boa Constrictor ▶

This sneaky snake coils around its prey and squeezes until it stops breathing. Then it swallows the prey whole. A boa can open its mouth wide enough to eat small pigs and monkeys! Boas are found mainly in Central and South America.

◀ Gila Monster

This big North American lizard is one of only two **venomous** lizards in the world. Eggs are one of the Gila monster's favorite foods. It uses its amazing sense of smell to find eggs even if they are buried.

Saltwater Crocodile ▶

It may look friendly, but don't let the smile fool you! This crocodile has the strongest bite of any animal. It has been known to leap up from the water to chomp a passing bird. It lives in the waters around Australia and Southeast Asia.

Do you want to meet some animals that are related to dinosaurs? You might be surprised to learn what they are!

Birds

Welcome to the bird exhibit. Scientists believe that birds evolved from dinosaurs millions of years ago. What makes a bird a bird? These animals all have feathers, a beak or bill, and wings. They lay eggs with hard shells. While all birds have wings, not all of them can fly. They come in many colors, shapes, and sizes!

Peacock

With his loud voice and bright feathers, the male peacock is hard to miss. The female, called a peahen, has mostly brown feathers to help her blend in with her surroundings.

Flamingo

What if your skin was the color of your favorite food? A flamingo's favorite food is brine shrimp. They eat so many of them that their feathers turn a pretty orangey pink!

Hummingbird

These tiny birds are some of the smallest in the world. Their eggs are tiny, too— about the size of a pea. Hummingbirds drink flower nectar and are the only birds that can fly backward.

Weaver Bird ▶

This little bird from Africa is an expert at weaving strands of grass together to make nests that look like upside-down baskets! The male bird makes the nest to get females to notice him.

Great Horned Owl

Owls are built for hunting at night. They have large eyes that allow them to see in almost complete darkness. Their ears can hear even the softest sounds. The feet, or talons, of the great horned owl are strong enough to crush bone.

Do you have a cat at home? We are ready to visit some very large cats. Follow me!

Big Cats

The big cats in this exhibit are all related to the **domestic** cats that we keep as pets. Can you see how they are similar? Like domestic cats, big cats have whiskers that can feel the smallest air movements from prey. Many wild cats purr. All of them are **carnivores**. Inside any cat's mouth you will notice a rough tongue that it uses to tear meat from bone and also for **grooming**.

▲ Jaguar
These cats live mainly in the rain forests of Central and South America and spend a lot of time around water. They enjoy swimming and are big and strong enough to catch and eat caimans—a type of alligator.

▲ Cougar
If you look at a cougar's face, you will notice that it looks a lot like a domestic cat's. That is because the cougar is the closest big-cat relative to house cats!

Snow ▶ Leopard

The thick fur of the snow leopard keeps it warm in the cold mountains of Asia. It has wide feet with fur underneath to help them grip icy surfaces and walk in deep snow.

Cheetah

This African cat is the fastest land animal. It can run up to 75 miles per hour—but only for very short distances.

Maybe instead of a cat, you have a hamster, gerbil, or mouse at home. They are all rodents—and they have lots of relatives in the wild. Let's meet some!

Rodents

What makes a rodent a rodent? All the animals in this group have two pairs of teeth—top and bottom—that never stop growing. The animal must gnaw or chew constantly to keep them short. Rodents are found on every continent except Antarctica. Almost half of all the mammals on earth are rodents! Our rodent exhibit has some interesting creatures to learn about.

◀ Porcupine

When being chased by a predator, a porcupine raises the spines, or quills, on its back. If a quill gets stuck in a predator's skin, it is very painful and does not come out easily.

Naked Mole Rat ▶

These animals live in long underground tunnels that they dig using their strong, giant teeth. It can't see well, but a naked mole rat has about 100 hairs on its body that help it feel its surroundings.

◀ Prairie Dog

When this North American rodent feels like it is in danger, it makes a sound like a dog barking. That is where its name comes from.

Capybara ▶

The largest of all the rodents, the capybara of South America is as much at home in the water as on land. It can run almost as fast as a horse, and can hold its breath for up to five minutes underwater.

◀ Beaver

Beavers use their strong teeth to cut down trees. They eat some of the wood and also use it to make large dams in a river. The dam is a pile of sticks and small trees that stops the water and makes a pond. The pond is where the beaver builds its home, which is known as a lodge.

*Most zoos don't have a lot of animals that live in the water, but we are lucky! Our zoo has a small **aquarium** where you can meet some underwater creatures. Right this way!*

At Home in the Water

Water covers more than two-thirds of our planet's surface. Some water habitats are salty (such as oceans and some rivers) and some have freshwater (such as most lakes and rivers). Many animals make these places their home. Some of them live in the water their whole lives, while others spend some time on land.

◀ Sea Lion

Built for swimming and hunting fish, a sea lion doesn't have legs— it has flippers! Sea lions can stay underwater for up to ten minutes without taking a breath.

Hawksbill ▶ Sea Turtle

Found near warm coral reefs, these turtles eat mostly sponges. Some of the sponges are poisonous to other animals, but they don't harm the sea turtles.

Reef Shark ▶

There are more than 400 kinds of sharks, and they are found in all the world's oceans. Large sharks have only two predators—other sharks and humans.

◀ Sea Otter

The playful sea otter spends most of its life in the ocean while it floats on the surface. It may use a rock to bash open a clamshell to get at the meat inside.

Beluga Whale ▶

This whale lives in the cold Arctic Ocean. Like other whales, belugas use sound to **communicate** with each other. They can whistle, click, and squeal. These sounds have earned it the nickname "sea canary."

You've met all our animals! Now would you like to meet some of the people who work at the zoo? They all have special jobs to do.

Who Works at the Zoo?

It takes many people doing different jobs to make sure all of our animals are healthy and happy. Would you like to work with the animals at a zoo one day? Which job would you like?

◀ Curator

Zoo curators make sure that exhibits are designed to be as much like an animal's natural home as possible. They also work to make sure that animals are grouped with other animals that will be good company for them.

▲ Nutritionist

The zoo nutritionist has one job—to make sure every animal gets the food it needs to stay healthy. There are usually several nutritionists and diet preparation people in each zoo.

▲ Veterinarian

Like people, animals get sick sometimes. When an alligator has a toothache, a toucan has a broken bill, or a giraffe is ready to have a baby, the veterinarians are there to help. Veterinarians are animal doctors who care for all the animals at the zoo.

◀ Zookeeper

There are many zookeepers like me at the zoo. Usually, each keeper has a type of animal or exhibit that he or she takes care of. The zookeeper works with the curators, nutritionists, and veterinarians to make sure the animals are healthy.

Zoo Educator ▶

People come to the zoo to learn. The educators are there to teach! They often talk to visitors about the animals. Sometimes they carry a parrot, owl, or snake with them for people to touch. Educators and **volunteers** can also help people find the exhibits they are looking for. Some zoos have programs that teach kids to be volunteers. Maybe you would like to volunteer at a zoo!

I hope you enjoyed your visit to the zoo today! I had a lot of fun bringing you to meet all the animals. Which one was your favorite?

Come visit us again soon!

Glossary

aquarium: A place where people can see live fish and water animals.

camouflage: Markings on the skin or fur of a creature that makes it blend in with its surroundings.

carnivore: A creature that eats only meat.

communicate: To use sounds, smells, or other signals to give information to another living thing.

continent: One of seven large pieces of land on earth (North America, South America, Europe, Asia, Africa, Australia, and Antarctica).

domestic: A type of animal that lives with people and is no longer wild.

exhibit: A space in a zoo where animals are grouped together for people to see.

extinct: When an animal becomes extinct, there are no longer any more of its kind living on earth.

grooming: Another name for cleaning fur, feathers, or skin.

habitat: A type of place that an animal lives in. Forests, jungles, and deserts are all habitats.

mammal: A type of animal that has fur and warm blood and makes milk for its young.

marsupial: A type of mammal that has a pouch on the female's stomach for carrying the babies.

polar regions: The cold areas surrounding the North and South poles.

predator: An animal that hunts other living things for food.

prey: An animal that is food for other animals.

species: A group of animals that have many things in common and which can produce offspring.

venomous: A venomous creature is one that makes venom—a poison that can harm other living things when injected.

volunteer: Someone who does work for free.

Model and Diorama Instructions

Complete one model at a time. Press out the pieces and arrange them as shown.
Using the numbers on the pictures here, match the slots and assemble your models.

African elephant

gorilla

peacock

trees

Hang the **chimpanzee** on a branch, and perch the **scarlet macaw** on top of the tree piece.

Stand the box lid and base upright. The inside scene will be the walls of your diorama. Attach the tree piece to the box lid as shown. Decorate the scene with reusable stickers, then set up your models and toys in front. Enjoy your own beautiful zoo!

Silver Dolphin Books

An imprint of the Baker & Taylor Publishing Group
10350 Barnes Canyon Road, San Diego, CA 92121
www.silverdolphinbooks.com

ISBN-13: 978-1-60710-909-9
ISBN-10: 1-60710-909-3
Manufactured, printed, and assembled in China.
1 2 3 4 5 17 16 15 14 13
FC1/11/13

ILLUSTRATION AND PHOTOGRAPH CREDITS
(t=top, b=bottom, m=middle, l=left, r=right, c=center)

Box Front: ©Peter Betts, ©Johannes Kornelius, ©leungchopin, ©Madien, ©neelsky, ©prapass, ©URRRA/Shutterstock.com
Front Cover: ©Marina Jay, ©neelsky/Shutterstock.com
Page 1: ©leungchopin/Shutterstock.com 1c;
Pages 2, 3: ©Hemera Technologies/photos.com 2tl; ©NorGal/Shutterstock.com 2t; ©Nadezhda1906/Shutterstock.com 3t;
Pages 4, 5: ©Intrepix/Shutterstock.com 4-5c (map); ©Ralf Juergen Kraft/Shutterstock.com 4 (beluga whale); ©stephen/Shutterstock.com 4 (sea lion); ©visceralimage/Shutterstock.com 4 (cougar); © fotofactory/Shutterstock.com 4 (beaver); ©KAMONRAT/Shutterstock.com 4 (macaw); ©Khoroshunova Olga/Shutterstock.com 4 (hawksbill sea turtle); ©Oleksiy Mark/Shutterstock.com 4 (toucan); ©Christian Musat/Shutterstock.com 4 (giant anteater); ©Johan Swanepoel/Shutterstock.com 4 (weaver bird); ©stephen/Shutterstock.com 4 (capybara); ©Nicram Sabod/Shutterstock.com 5 (puffin); ©andamanec/Shutterstock.com 5 (polar bear); ©Stu Porter/Shutterstock.com 5 (lion); © jps/Shutterstock.com 5 (hippopotamus); ©Richard Peterson/Shutterstock.com 5 (elephant) ; ©Stu Porter/Shutterstock.com 5 (cheetah); ©Roberto Caucino/Shutterstock.com 5 (lemur); ©cbpix/Shutterstock.com 5 (reef shark); ©Artush/Shutterstock.com 5 (snow leopard); ©neelsky/Shutterstock.com 5 (tiger); ©leungchopan/Shutterstock.com 5 (panda); ©Rob Francis/Shutterstock.com 5 (sloth bear); ©Greenfire/Shutterstock.com 5 (orangutan); ©Anna Kucherova/Shutterstock.com 5 (komodo dragon); ©worldswildlifewonders/Shutterstock.com 5 (koala); ©worldswildlifewonders/Shutterstock.com 5 (platypus); ©Photodynamic/Shutterstock.com 5 (penguin);
Pages 6, 7: ©lsantilli/Shutterstock.com 6tl; ©Tomaz Kunst/Shutterstock.com 6bl; ©EcoPrint/Shutterstock.com 6br; ©BOONCHUAY PROMJIAM/Shutterstock.com 7tl; ©Kairos69/Shutterstock.com 7tr; ©Pal Teravagimov/Shutterstock.com 7bl;
Pages 8, 9: ©Oleksiy Mark/Shutterstock.com 8tl; ©Shvak/Shutterstock.com 8c; ©KAMONRAT/Shutterstock.com 8r; ©Christian Musat/Shutterstock.com 9tr; ©worldswildlifewonders/Shutterstock.com 9tl; ©Santi Rodriguez/Shutterstock.com 9br;
Pages 10, 11: ©silver-john/Shutterstock.com 10l; ©neelsky/Shutterstock.com 10r; ©Anna Kucherova/Shutterstock.com 11tl; ©Nagel Photography/Shutterstock.com 11r; ©neelsky/Shutterstock.com 11br;
Pages 12, 13: ©worldswildlifewonders/Shutterstock.com 12l; ©Kjuuurs/Shutterstock.com 12r; ©worldswildlifewonders/Shutterstock.com 13l; ©Susan Flashman/Shutterstock.com 13tr; ©Shane White/Shutterstock.com 13br;
Pages 14, 15: ©andamanec/Shutterstock.com 14l; ©Nicram Sabod/Shutterstock.com 14r; ©Vladimir Melnik/Shutterstock.com 15l; ©perlphoto/Shutterstock.com 15tr; ©Photodynamic/Shutterstock.com 15br;
Pages 16, 17: ©Kjersti Joergensen/Shutterstock.com 16l; ©Elliot Hurwitt/Shutterstock.com 16r; ©MarclSchauer/Shutterstock.com 17l; ©PhotoBarmaley/Shutterstock.com 17tc; ©Roberto Caucino/Shutterstock.com 17tr; ©Aleksei Verhovski/Shutterstock.com 17br;
Pages 18, 19: ©larus/Shutterstock.com 18l; ©EcoPrint/Shutterstock.com 18r; ©reptiles4all/Shutterstock.com 19l; ©Roy Palmer/Shutterstock.com 19tr; ©Audrey Snider-Bell/Shutterstock.com 19br;
Pages 20, 21: ©apiguide/Shutterstock.com 20l; ©pr2is/Shutterstock.com 20r; ©Steve Byland/Shutterstock.com 21tl; ©mlorenz/Shutterstock.com 21tr; ©Johan Swanepoel/Shutterstock.com 21bl;
Pages 22, 23: ©Krzysztof Wiktor/Shutterstock.com 22l; ©visceralimage/Shutterstock.com 22r; ©Ian Rentoul/Shutterstock.com 23t; ©photobar/Shutterstock.com 23b;
Pages 24, 25: ©tratong/Shutterstock.com 24l; ©belizar/Shutterstock.com 24r; ©Henk Bentlage/Shutterstock.com 25tl; ©stephen/Shutterstock.com 25tr; ©fotofactory/Shutterstock.com 25bl;
Pages 26, 27: ©stephen/Shutterstock.com 26l; ©Achimdiver/Shutterstock.com 26r; ©cbpix/Shutterstock.com 27tr; ©Dan Bannister/Shutterstock.com 27tl; ©Miles Away Photography/Shutterstock.com 27br;
Pages 28, 29: ©iStockphoto.com/kali9 28tl; ©Alina555/iphoto.com and ©Sam DCruz/Shutterstock.com 28bl; © Bork/Shutterstock.com 28tr; ©RadioFan at en.wikipedia (http://enwikipedia.org)/Wikimedia Commons/CC-BY-SA-3.0 29tl; ©ROBERTO ZILLI/Shutterstock.com 29tr; ©Hemera Technologies/photos.com 29bl;
Diorama Imagery: ©Dhoxax, Joanne Harris and Daniel Bubnich, Marci Paravia, Stu Porter, Kschotanus/CC-BY-SA-3.0 (http://creativecommons.org/licenses/by-sa/3.0/)
Stickers: ©Ekaterina V. Borisova, ©ehtesham, ©Eric Gevaert, ©Marina Jay, ©KAMONRAT, ©Oleksiy Mark, ©Stu Porter, ©Patrick Rolands, ©MarclSchauer, ©Pal Teravagimov, ©prapass, ©robinimages2013, ©Vaclav Volrab
Models: ©apiguide, ©Shawn Hempel, ©KAMONRAT, ©Alexandra Lande, ©Marci Paravia, ©Richard Peterson, ©Smileus, ©Sergey Uryadnikov/Shutterstock.com